Gunited States

Steven Mooney

Gunited States © 2023, 2026 Steven Mooney

This edition supersedes the volume published in 2023 by
Last Word Press

First Draft2Digtal Edition

All rights reserved. No parts of this publication may be reproduced, stored in a retrieval system, or transmitted in any form or by any means, electronic, mechanical, photocopying, recording, or otherwise, without the prior written permission of the copyright owner.

Cover Image: Gun Country by Michael Murphy

Book Design and Editing by Peter Mooney

"We need to start treating gun violence like the public health crisis it is."
—Cory Booker

"The Second Amendment is not a suicide pact."
—Former Chief Justice Warren Burger

"I hate war as only a soldier who has lived it can, only as one who has seen its brutality, its futility, its stupidity."
—Dwight David Eisenhour

Contents

Introduction 1
Mandate Handshake Reveal 2
Gunplay Insurgency 4
Artful Heartless Freedom 5
American Gun-lust Quatrains 7
Rust, Lasting Blood of Naval War 8
Bullet Head Bullet Brain 11
American Blood Relative 13
The Target 15
Flintlock Membrane: An Immodest Proposal 16
Editing the National Anthem 19
Veteran of Peace 20
A Nation of Dupes? 23

Gunited States
Part One: War at Our Core 33
Part Two: Dream World Interlude 42
Part Three: Gore in Our Lore 45

Afterword 54

Introduction

Gather 'round children and you will hear

How a love of guns drew our false frontier,

Where truth & lies were swapped & dealt by

The likes of Buffalo Bill & Teddy Roosevelt,

We've built an industry in factory & in song

As vibrant as our willingness to play along;

We march to a myth that's at least as greedy

As our need to Feed that natal Beast,

We each resemble at our best a zealot

Dressed in a dynamite vest as we shed

Ours and others blood to fill the gutters

When and wherever Old Glory flutters.

Mandate Handshake Reveal

The solution to our gun violence
    is first of all one of balance:
We must be broad minded or not
    seduced or entranced by platitudes, for
Only then may we commence to practice
Equal measures of love & tolerance.

With tolerance we open that house of doors,
    Beware each door screams its own horrors:
    Weak laws! Poverty!
    Homelife instability!
    Mental health! Drugs!
    Ineqaulity! All haunt its corridors;
        but of couse there are others,
    Doors further still, but these remain
        hot-button issues that will circle the drain
            with come-together Americans in action!

Sit down with me,
let's talk awhile,
share a drink or coffee or tea, by all means
share a smile. We have a pressing problem to solve,
    one step at a time,
        to stop a turntable's enabled rotation.
Oh, you're on *that* side of the aisle? Well, I respect
your freedom (earned) to be so inclined, and once we
get to talking and find we have some things in common,

    thanks for understanding my frame of mind, or
    we openly agree we don't like each other,
but see the Greater Problem
    and our shake-hands agree
the decks are cleared for action
Clinical studies are not enough, but
    Town Hall meetings would help to
address each Hydra head's enormity!

Standing in the way of gun reform
In a nation divided by ideology,
Political propaganda as the norm
Threatens us all with a faux mythology;

Bury the hatchet with the rhetoric and spin!
We haven't done that yet, let us give it a try,
Through trial and error, together we'll win and
Answers to How will best most questions of Why.

Gunplay Insurgency

Anarchy in slow motion

   Predictable yet random,

Ungoverned yet groomed,

   Destructive yet prescriptive,

Day in and day out,

   Week by week, cheek by jowl,

Month upon grisly month

Time stilled only for the targets,

   Tolerated amid the intolerant,

Emergent yet perpetual,

   Moving slowly yet ever leading,

Crawling apace to set the stage for

   A nation's internal bleeding,

Witnessed by our managed rage;

   Each individual actor

Enjoins a collective act of nihilism;

   For everything we defile,

   We are all in denial!

Artful Heartless Freedom

America, you have lost your Soul,
From the willing proliferation of war,
Korea, Vietnam, Iraq (more in store)
To greed's incessant need of More, More,
And a political system rife with rancor
As integrity & respect are flushed whole;
America, you have lost your Soul!

America, you have lost your Soul,
In every town and city the homeless
Attest our unwillingness to redress a
Societal pandemic without love or caress,
In a political system's blame game mess
Where compassion & care are flushed whole;
America, you have lost your soul!

America, you have lost your soul to a
religion of ballistics & the godly gun,
Backed by Wild West mythology's lengthy run,
Like Russian Roulette with the cylinders spun,
Children, our parents, we will shoot anyone
Where sanctity of life plays a slogan's role;
America, you have lost your Soul!

America, you have lost your soul!
If ever you had one: looking back at our
Genocidal treatment of red man and black,
It's both ethics & morals that we lack, from
Jim Crow laws to police murders we track
Prejudice & overt intolerance on the attack;
The question then is beggared: what is to be
Our goal in a nation that has lost its Soul?

Americans in love with racial hatred
Denounce Democracy as Outdated, as
January 6 in infamy revealed, their plan
Inspired by a convicted felon con man.
Guns & God bolster a whites-only vow
To usurp progress and thereby allow
Freedom's endgame to take its toll by
Destroying Liberty and gutting its Soul.

Better Americans wield the active tool
That guides day to day the Golden Rule and
Embraces strength in diversity's melting pot
Rejoicing in our heritage of liberty polyglot.
Folks in whom compassion and empathy run
Defy our freedoms being willfully undone, and
Take to the streets with the placard, not the gun,
Each to play their patriot Thomas Paine role:
Americans regain and restore our nation's Soul!

American Gun-lust Quatrains

Savage bloodlust never satisfied:
Take the remake of Bonnie and Clyde,
Fifty-some years separate the flicks of
Gun-lust psychopaths loose in the sticks.

Selling the story's ever the goal
As long as actors will play the role,
Costner and Harrelson have their say,
Different from Beatty, Dunaway,

No need to see it from the other side:
Old lawmen midlife crisis implied,
Perspective gives it no other path
But leads to the tale-ending bloodbath,

KILLING is what it's all about:
Gun lust carries cinematic clout,
Mainly when massed firepower prevails
Over Ethics in box office sales.

Rust, Lasting Blood of Naval War

Part One

We, all of us, lost that war,
The Second World, those
Victory parades now archaic
Stravinsky sepia news reels of
Triumphant allure,
Allies rolling to victory sure
Over Fascist horror leads
Eventually to reveal
The United Nations
Which now appoints us to
Our collective guilt:
Recipients of 6,338 ships
Sunk in the conflict, brim
Full up with gas, diesel, oil,
Lubricants & assorted gunk
NOAA estimates at approx.
Fifteen million tons in tanks
Just about eaten through - fifteen million tons
multiplied by seventy-five give or take years of
Rust gives us just that: 6,338 Ocean
Floor fuel bunkers soon to spew, to
Release into already endangered seas.

Norway acts alone of all the
Nations united or not, they are
Pumping out the oil in a race with
Catastrophe which will do more

Than despoil their coastal and
Estuarine land, their nation's
Health is their requisite core

While the rest of we, all of us:
Either generally ignorant of
The crisis or if it's known have
Adapted a do-nothing wait & see
Tautology like a new chapter in
Some climate change Comic Book.

The Billions of dollars squandered on
U.S. Militarism should be used to address
Our own collusion in this colossal mess.
Until then, how about more metaphor:
We all are the stilled screws of sunken war ships,
Inheritors of might makes right Methuselahs!

Part Two

Out of 20,000 documented sunken wrecks in
U. S. waters, 50-odd hold multimillion crude
Oil gallons. From but a select few has the
Coastguard and U.S. Navy extracted oil,
Gasoline, and in turn paints, cleaners, and
Solvents, refrigerants, older nasties like
Benzene, asbestos, PCBs, but proving that
Wealthy nations can come to grips with sunken ships.

The most famous leaking ship is the U. S. S. Arizona,
Roughly a gallon of oil daily since 1941 so dated.
A spill that's estimated to continue
Unabated for 500 years; so, the question must
Be asked, when will national bereavement end
Its arrears in worship of the doomed entombed?
Branded grief for the dead must be ameliorated
That we may take oil from like vessels so ill-fated!

Let us inquire of sailors killed by torpedo and shell
If they feel disrespected or dishonored for their toil
Between the gates of Heaven and the shafts of Hell,
That we'd disturb their peace to obtain all that oil –
The bones are long gone; that's no shocker given
Microbes and creatures in Davy Jones Locker.
So, let us salvage pollutants, gather up steel,
But let memorials stand as war's Lone Reveal!

Upon the sea we toss a wreath, offer up words of
Something bequeath, then sail off toward
Extant concerns, as it should be until
The next year's routine anniversary.
>   Cleaning the oceans must be our locus,
>   Leave the dead to tributes, statues, plaques.
>   Great grandkids will champion our keen focus
>   On confronting wars' fallout through selfless acts.

Bullet Head Bullet Brain

Bullet head Bullet brain, Bullet fed Bullet grain,
Bullet sire Bullet spawn, Bullet night to Bullet dawn,
Bullet school to Bullet degree, Bullet is cool
    We {don't all} agree,
Bullet reap and Bullet sow, Oh, how they leap to mow
    Down kids in rows,
Bullet movie Bullet mall, oh so groovy, fun for all!
Bullet burger Bullet work, only a jerk calls it murder.
What Bullet brings is Freedom Ring let Freedom Ring
Like bells, the echoed shot for it's not free if it ain't got
the Blood, White & Blue of Bullet me and Bullet you!
Bullet hide and Bullet seek, Bullet finds the humble, meek,
Bullet rich Bullet poor, Bullet gets past any door,
Bullet meal Bullet feast, Bullet zeal West and East,
Bullet show Bullet tell, Bullet knows very well
that Bullet praise and Bullet mouth talk
Bullet grace in North and South, for
Bullet high and Bullet low,
Bullet vies for best in show, whether
Bullet crime or Bullet cop,
Bullet time comes out on top, for
Bullet woman and Bullet man,
It is Bullet omens we understand, with
Bullet Father, Bullet Son, and Bullet Holy Ghost,
Bullet gather as Bullet one with Bullet heavenly host:

Our Bullet who art in heaven,
Hallowed be thy Bullet,
Thy Bullet come,
Thy Bullet be done
On earth as it is in Bullet, and give us this day
Our daily Bullet, and forgive those Bullets
That trespass against other Bullets, and
Lead no Bullet into temptation, and
Deliver Bullet from evil, for thy
Bullet is the Kingdom Bullet,
The Glory Bullet, and the (steel-jacketed)
Power Bullet, forever and ever, and Lord,
Bullet is another kind of bomb, so we sing this
Our anthem with aplomb!
    Amen is heard submerged in coughs,
    In barks and stutters amid the troughs;
    Pew homilies traded like hoots and calls
Echoing in those once-sanctified walls, the
Cries of murdered children!

~ * ~

Only when we replace the lethal bullet
With the bullet of Love,
Will we rise above and thereby condemn
Our homegrown culture-wide mayhem!

American Blood Relative

Oscillating, mouthing, the
Multitudes surge
Screaming, flailing,
Get out the word:
Without guns it'd be
Breakbone sticks wailing
A nation's lubricant cries
Its common failing;
Basal hatred belies
Freedom sloganeering
Land of the free:
Free to shoot
Credulous citizenry,
Home of the brave:
Spartan invertebrate
Cold-blooded spillage's
Intolerance engineering,
Revolving repugnant
Sectarian prerogative
Urge to purge neighborhoods,
Ethnic, Semitic, anyone
Seen as the Other. Ours is
A nation disunited by
An American institution
Like no other
Not like jazz, not like faith, but
Not unlike a ghastly sport, for
Nothing unifies us more
Than using deadly force to
Keep scores or settle them.

Through semantic change
We may yet turn from
Howling like apes:
Alter the noun guns to the
Phrase, *Mass Murder*, for
Who shop genocide?
Who carry-conceal horrific?
What national organization
Promote mass murder?
What Constitutional Amendment
Assure the people bloodbaths?
"So, what's your position on
Mass Murder, Congressman,
Pastor, Imam, mom and dad,
Working stiffs good and bad,
Spread across the land?"
One person shot dead
Kills something in us all,
Making us less human, and
The American Dream
Is ever the first to fall.

The Target

Local city councils and their mayors
Aiming to curb rampant gun killing
Too often are left with thoughts & prayers
When reforms are killed off by the willing,

Gun safety measures are ever opposed
By gun rights lobbies & ditto-head sops
That often prevail as Drives get hosed,
Falling to that chestnut, hire more cops,

Blind faith funnels gun lust's robust rooting,
No act too flamboyant to fuel their drive,
For the growing numbers of mass shootings
Recorded by Gun Violence Archive,

Now, some beat the drum for civil war,
An oxymoronic boiler plate,
One with intolerance at its core
That praises the gun as how to relate,

A nation reeling from deadly disease,
Seeking relief from the pandemic
Must come together to find release
By making tolerance systemic.

Flintlock Membrane: An Immodest Proposal

Let us restrict civilian gun owners to
    the weapons used in the period in which the
Second Amendment to the United States Constitution
    was written and so satisfy

Why we are so smitten and vexed

from taking a sentence out of its context!

    I'd go for it. You?

That amendment is out of step

    With the times,

Yet its context we hold to be true

    For *ALL TIME*. Thus, let us restrict

One flintlock musket per family member,

    Ditto one flintlock pistol, and for each a
Single sack of powder and a sack of Sack too!

The framers could not have imagined
Gatling Guns of a century hence, much less today's
Hand-held household garden-variety automatic
Butchery tools turned loose daily in
Places of worship and commerce,
    and in our schools!

    Our forefathers knew nothing of machine guns.
    What they meant by "arms" was

the Assault Weapon of Concord and Lexington, of
Fort Ticonderoga and Breeds Hill; and later still of
Latter day Minutemen betrayed and made poor farmer
hellion and fought in Daniel Shays Rebellion.

The "shot heard 'round the world" was

One Shot!

(Not that staccato rip from a banana clip!)

Let us examine how the flintlock rifle is prepped for the next

Single Shot:

- Use a clean cloth to wipe the lock
- Check the flint for it must be sharp, if needed knap a new edge (but don't try it in the dark)
- Use the vent prick to clear the touch hole
- Swab the barrel but don't use your shirt, use a clean patch, free of dirt
- Pull the lock to half cock
- Pinch a cartridge from the cartouche, bring it to your mouth after oxygen debouche
- Tear the cartridge with your teeth (denture bearers may need relief)
- Pour priming powder to fill half the flash pan, away from the touch hole (too much powder may act like a fuse and slow ignition)

- Close the pan
- Stand the rifle on its stock with muzzle facing the sky (Don't look into the bore and don't ask why)
- Pour the charge down the barrel (powder measure)
- Start the ball down the muzzle over a lubricated patch
- Use the short starter first, long starter second, and the ramrod to seat the ball firmly against the charge
- Set the hammer to full cock and take aim
- Squeeze the trigger and hold aim until the BLAST!

By such process, muskets will muzzle
    Mass Killings and they will pass in decline as
Orders for ramrod and nipple wrench amass and
    Redefine how responders take aim on the
Muzzleloading black-powder active shooter.
    We'll then party with fellow citizen gun lovers,
    Glossing their shine in context line by line.

Editing the National Anthem

Gun lust is the progenitor of the
military-industrial brain trust, and

Father and daughter is how best to
view them to understand slaughter:

Might makes Right descends its lineage
through the heart of (our) cultural plight,

Yet tradition boasts of second sight and
promotes reviews with each rendition,

Sing McHenry, Yorktown, San Juan Hill:
fluttering flags and the glory they bring,

While blind eyes are turned toward centillion
budgets supporting glory of another kind,

Gun lust, a North American pandemic sewn
in our social fabric as though it's a must, as

Though killing kids in our schools and abroad
is the birthright and pledge of the willing;
Wildfire raging creates cyclones of doom
before which all will be consumed or expire.

Veteran of Peace

To my ex-military friends, this may help you
Grasp the swerve of those who chose not to serve
in the armed forces:
We're not veterans of war. We are veterans of Peace!
Some of us left home as teenagers, kicked out by our fathers
who refused to acknowledge the Times a changing.
For some of us, that footloose freedom was an adventure.
For others, there was the fear we
Might get drafted and sent to a
War by Warriors crafted.
We loved our country, but we didn't believe
the hype over 'Nam' communism stereotype.
We hoped like hell we wouldn't be sent to
The four corners of the world
      to kill people
That Richard Nixon said a threat to the
Security of the greatest nation on earth but
For many, Dean Smith's Four Corners was good enough!
For others, it was Positively 4th Street.
We heard Dylan, Ochs, Baez, but listening otherwise
Their antiwar songs became our anthems.
We made lasting friendships in the peace movement.
We made brothers and sisters.
We made love, not war.
We joined hands in a nationwide movement.

We cheered on our heroes such as Allen Ginsberg, the Catonsville Nine, the Berrigans.

We attended teach-ins against the war.

We attended antiwar protest planning sessions.

We marched (down Main Street) in Moratorium parades.

We attended antiwar protests that were peaceful.

We attended antiwar protests that were not peaceful.

No one I knew behaved violently, but

We got caught up in it.

We got chased by riot-squad cops.

We got walled in by phalanx of Billy clubs.

Some of us got tear-gassed, others got beaten.

Some of us got arrested.

Some of us got interviewed.

Some of us ducked into alleys for a breather, or a joint.

We participated in time-honored pacifist rituals

Strengthening our bonds and camaraderie.

We mourned, as one, over the Kent State murders.

We burned, as one, with immolated Buddhist monks.

We reeled in horror over the My Lai Massacre, then in stunned silence when there was no accountability:

Killers ran free from their butchery.

We felt as one for civilians, as well for combatants

Caught in the haze of Agent Orange.

Most importantly,

We saw our collective action

Help to end that stupid war's intractable infraction.

We empathized with those among us

Who got drafted and went along with it,

Like a buddy of mine who lost his deferment.

He told them he intended to return to complete an

Engineering degree, so they made him a clerk in

An engineering battalion, and he spent his war

Typing and delivering the mail.

The coolest thing is that he doesn't brag about grand

Service performed for his country; no, he put it all behind him while he

finished growing up (warzones' stunted hormones).

    We met again at the Desert Storm antiwar rally

    (So many more since it is tough to tally),

    The faces of our family, true patriots all, were

    Gathered again and freezing on the National Mall.

    We didn't stop that war, but hey, at least we tried,

    Burnishing to gloss America's Other Side bona fide.

A Nation of Dupes?

Support the troops we hear people say!
Repeated in media, on air, and everywhere! I say,
       Hell Yeah, as related to some Morally justified
Lethal threat! Attack by an Identifiable Nation or
Nation State the likes of which
We haven't seen since 1941, December 7.
       Someone always rolls out their lament of 911—but
          That act we brought upon ourselves:
          Tank treads in a Holy Land we
          Never Bothered to understand!
In our reverent denial
Let us make public what we've defiled: Senseless Expense
Draws queries to the gates of Defense Contractors
       LOCKED!
The public has been locked out but no less
Loaded into this juggernaut we must attest, only
Our sweat, known as tax dollars, is allowed access:

The billion-dollar military contract lobby
Operationally independent of public vent
Banks on foreign excursions for their hobby
Of testing their toys where our forces are sent:

1961

Dwight David Eisenhour spoke of the threat of
Keeping the military-industrial pet, but those who
Didn't listen were already banked up, ready to ignore
The powerless people for the lucrative power of WAR:

The Arsenal of Democracy is the larder of weaponry;
Unending war spending has prompted our global
adventurism and brought us to where we are today,
What a Public Shuck funding Forever War run Amok.

We the people number among how many willing dupes
Waving flags, giving lip service support the troops no
matter what, no matter where they go, but Hey, turn on
the TV we don't want to miss our favorite show!

> Many of our foreign martial actions were eclipsed by
> movies, TV shows and commercial advert distractions.

Dominican Republic   1965

On bogus proof of a Commie Bogie man, we invaded
to back a right-wing Junta's plan but up the island chain
James Bond fought S.P.E.C.T.R.E. on the old Spanish Main,
and the hills were alive with The Sound of Music amid
Dr. Zhivago and the Cincinnati Kid, and Volkswagen
urged us, Think Small. Other ads said Put a tiger
in your tank and See the USA in your Chevrolet.

Lebanon   1982   / Grenada   1983

For all the public cared, our peacekeeping mission sent
Marines to the valley of the jolly ho-ho-ho Green Giant.
Stroh's is spoken here. Give me a break, give me a break,
Break off a piece of that Kit Kat bar, sang the compliant.
/
   On Fantasy Island, Toucan Sam topped
   Uncle Sam as did Cap'n Crunch, and General Mills
   issued orders with a Snap, Crackle, Pop, Rice Krispies!
   Oh what a feeling to drive-Toyota. Tide's in, dirt's out.

Persian Gulf   1988

The best part of waking up is Folgers in your cup.
What's a Persian gulf, said Palmolive's Manicurist Madge
with the dishpan hands as she reached out for Bounty, the
Quicker Picker Upper. Mr. Whipple squeezed the Charmin
and Poppin' Fresh, the Pillsbury Doughboy was poked. On
the next commercial Joe Camel nonchalantly smoked.

Panama   1989

Our attack on Panama was top of the news but
Operation Just Cause lost out to addictive views of
Wheel of Fortune, The Price is Right, and Santa Claus.
While our planes strafed barrios killing civilians by scores,
We went Christmas shopping in malls and department stores.

Kuwait, Iraq   1991

Iraq invading Kuwait prompted us to permeate
the region in the clamor for all that oil through a
story of our own induction that suckered nations
over invented weapons of mass destruction. But also
on the attack were the Pep Boys Manny, Moe, and Jack.
On TV bogs, Bud, Weis, and Er, Anheuser-Busch frogs
cleared the air during Who Wants to be a Millionaire!

Somalia   1993

Sounded like a sleep aid: 'When a day's hectic tensions
wanna follow ya, you'll rest easy with Somalia.' Or was it
Army Rangers in some Middle East game or Mrs. Butterworth's
maiden name, or Mr. Peanut in the shell, or was it Gidget
the chihuahua rasping, ¡Yo Quiero Taco Bell?
No matter, Plop, plop, fiz, fiz, Oh what a relief it is!

Haiti   1994

Some of our military adventures gain attention.
We responded to a coup d'état in which elected
officials were shot as a matter of convention,
but who really gave a swot, well, not Little Debbie,
and not Mr. Clean, not Snuggle Bear or Woodsy Owl
if you know what I mean. Oh I wish I were an Oscar Mayer
Wiener, that is what I'd really like to be, Cuz if I were an
Oscar Mayer Wiener, everyone would be in love with me.

Bosnia   1994, 1995   Kosovo   1999

How did ethnic war in the Balkans stack up against
Everybody Loves Raymond and Sponge Bob Square Pants? Well,
a few more questions: How about a nice Hawaiian Punch?
Pardon me, do you have any Grey Poupon? No, but we've
got Friends, Frasier, Will & Grace, X-Files, West Wing & Stargate.
Nationwide is on your side.

   Then, the acts of Nine-Eleven-Two thousand One awoke us
from our TV trance of sitcoms, prime time dramas, and
soap opera romance, soggy to their core. From our dens
living rooms, and offices and more, we all went to war:

Afghanistan   2002, 2003, 2004
The protest March on D.C., "End the Madness" gathered
Only a few thousand, while on it went, year upon year,
2005 …… 2009, but in 2010 a singular event hit home when
Two dozen Afghanis in a wedding party were butchered by
Drone as the Apogee of Depravity we Condone!
   On and on it went, 2011 and 2012*, 2013, and 2014 ……
{Ho-hum beat that lost-interest drum as IEDs and convoy kills
paled before Stateside TV Network thrills} …………2021!

In Afghanistan, what was our mission?
    In Iraq, we acted on lies of nuclear fission,
        but Afghanistan?
Well, it's complicated ya understand ...
    You add Isis & Al Queda and
        then Multiply by X Warlords
divided by public attention span = Taliban

But when the going got tough (* way back when),
Jon and Joan Public had had enough and fell into a lull
When the fighting overseas paled before Boob Tube/Internet priorities:
Facebook, Nip/Tuck, Chuck, Scrubs, Monk, House, Reba, Dexter,
Heroes, Smallville, Survivor & more we just had to see:
Gossip Girl, Girlfriends, and Glee; 30 Rock, Supernatural, and
Modern Family; Mad Men, Parks & Rec and Grey's Anatomy;
Desperate Housewives, American Idol and The O.C.;
Dr. Who, The Wire, and Ugly Betty.
And the Energizer Bunny beating his drum was too funny!
Aren't you glad you use Dial? Don't you wish everybody did?
    Like a good neighbor, State Farm is there.
    What would you do for a Klondike Bar?

Meanwhile, the Taliban attacked
and somewhat spoiled the invasion
Before melting into the hills.

In Kabul our sponsored corruption spread
as civilians suffered & fighters tallied kills until
   one U.S. President had the balls to say Enough!
     Once and for All!
  A chaotic withdrawal his critics would exclaim,
   as though tidy ends could make amends and
bend the essential achievement's aim, to shut the door on our
    World-beater theatre of forever war!

Several years later we've awakened once again from
Our sloth like slumber of game show mentality,
Celebrity worship, and prize money plunder, like a
Time bomb ticking, our asses were ripe for a kicking!
  But who'd have thunk our cities would be attacked by
  Minions of a megalomaniac, bent by a sitting President?
L. A., Chicago, Washington, D.C., Portland, Memphis, NYC,
Oakland, St. Louis, New Orleans, San Francisco, Minneapolis ... 2025, 2026

Deployment of our National Guard
Into these American cities drew
Far more contempt than it did pity,
Prompted by the invented canard of
Its weakling commander in chief,
Hoist upon his own bloated petard.
Hell bent on his deportation quota
Goon squads run a reign of terror rota!

ICE today is the Klan rebranded as Secret Police
~ incarnate, craven, evil ~ that must be
disbanded and abolished
now that they have played their hand
killing Americans, then calling 'em terrorists!

A male nurse, and a mother of three
Exercising their 1st Amendment rights,
Murdered while observing peacefully are
Martyred for upholding Democracy!
Citizens Alex Pretti and Renee Good
Gunned down in a blitz of insanity will
Live to guide America to right this profanity!

In criminal law officers go armed, but for
Civil law, such as Immigration (or what that pretends),
Carrying guns makes no sense! Nor does tactical gear, worn
Only to inspire fear, but ICE/CBP abusive events made a
Paul Revere out of each one of the Twin City residents,
Spreading the message by word and by whistle, from
Kitchens and nooks and living rooms and dens
Communities became neighborhood bucket brigades to
Redress for Justice to make amends and halt the
Destruction of their beloved Republic!

Held hostage by bone spur-driven top-down Racism,
Uncle Sam points and says, "I Want You to Fight Fascism!"

Caribbean Sea, Arabian Gulf   2025, 2026

Claiming water taxis are narco boats and slaughtering
Those on board, the U.S. Navy has declared itself
Undisputed Caribbean Sea Lord! With Venezuelan oil
In its sights, we witness hubris trample human rights!
    America now beats the drums of war
        Strutting forth the militarist whore. And to underscore,
            We join the Genocidal Israelis to attack Iran!
On a Saturday, 'Monday' in the Middle East, a ballistic missile,
                Mark of the Beast,
        Slaughtered a school full of children!

Is another Afghanistan the plan? More Wait & See Strategy?
It's a war that can only be won on spin, a ruse to enact the
War Powers Act at White House whim and further erase the
                Rule of Law.

{Here, the Omniscient Editor
Throws her hat into
The ring of the predator,
And along with her we sing}:

        The Flying Fortress is our God
Oh the B-52 full of bombs and rockets too
        Flying from us all the way to you,
Winged death skull Angelic Voodoo, and an
        Aimed personal memo from

Uncle Sam , and a Personal message from
General Electric, and a
    Personal message from
General Dynamics, and a
    Personal message from
General Honeywell,
    and bromide text re:
Chairman General Merchandise:
    Freedom Ordnance wishing you well
        Forever in Hell,
    Wherever Whoever you are,
A Gift from us at the Death Star,
    Lovely Gift from the Death Star!

Please thank Moloch for your fate, by Bullet bread
All will be fed, give us lord our daily dead.

In worship we talk to God
Fingers laced,
Eyes tight shut,
How evil rides Unshod, yet seek Beneficent yields to
Anoint the killing-fields we've sown:
Armed Forces in 187 countries: Toy deploy Oh Boy!

And yet, between our wars we search for Love
To bandage wounds and salve our souls,
Like the song says, the world has so little of:
Why not exchange it for our bloodletting roles:

The theater of War as juicy plum:
Attracting both talented and ham actors
Wrapped in the flag and beating the drum
Roles are bid by the top contractors
That strive to make a name as players
On the world stage as deadly assayers:

In order to promote militarism,
One must practice at the art of war,
A practice that's made perfect through schism
As Death learns its lines, rehearses the score.

The chorus of veterans of course has the urge
To sing how proud they are to have served;
But the national anthem becomes a dirge
About the fate of the undeserved (*civilian collateral damage*)

Organized violence rends asunder,
Ruin, slaughter with carnage deployed
But pales next to that glorious thunder
Until players or the play's destroyed

One heady slogan is, Give Peace a Chance!
We must empower it to our core;
With climate now changing the world's balance,
And stop paying for the militarist whore!

Gunited States
Part One: War at Our Core

"That whole damn war business is about nine-hundred-and-ninety-nine parts diarrhea to one part glory." —Walt Whitman

That Lone Blind Eye of the Eagle

Faces the olive branch it cannot see,

Arrows like bombs in bomb bay doors,

    Symbolic of militarist whores!

We do little to stop forever wars

Because we love forever wars

    We militarist whores;

Our foreign policy underscores how

We create discord then settle scores,

    We militarist whores!

It is celebrity and shopping and

Money more Money more Money

Our TV-enchanted culture adores,

    We militarist whores;

We brew hatred and then blame others

For our self-inflicted sores, while to

Arms manufacturers our money pours,

    We militarist whores! Yet our Gun Culture is one that Adores *wild* West & Gang-bred gun love lore,

    We Gang Bang whores!

We bring slaughter to our communities, to
Our churches Our mosques Our schools Our stores,
    We are all conspirators! We
Decry and beseech and bemoan
The Homegrown Terror that *We* Own,
The cyclical murder that We have Sown,
       yet deny
We've opened those doors,
    We shoot-em-up whores;
One day per year our obeisance
We declare: The rockets' red glare
Bombs bursting in air,
Gave proof through the night that
       Our flag was still there:
A Symbol of Wars, so kneel, sit or stand as
Our national anthem soars, for we are all contributors:

    (There is no other nation on Earth
    Spends so ravishingly on killing,
    No expense spared for what it's worth:
    Our taxes take care of the billing
    While untaxed wealth rejoices in mirth
    Taking grand profits from the willing)

How did we come to be such whores?
Let us view a sampler of assorted rifle bores:

The "Indian Problem:"
Vacuum up the Cherokee to make room for
Racist hegemony: the saddest chapter in
Our national biography also footnotes our
Whitewashed textbook hagiography;

The Mexican War:
Annexation without Representation or
Destiny manifest at Others' Behest
{see Philippine-American War} at its nexus an added U.S. state;

The American Civil War:
Slavery; Bloodshed; Bravery & Knavery:
"Reconstruction" led by a Racist President
Who saw the Freed Man as outlaw;

The Indian Wars:
Prep slaughter of *savages* by Westward Ho avarice
(Manifest Destiny Treasury Chest) made pulp
Fiction of the white man's side which in time
Became American history's point of pride

> (Teddy Roosevelt's Black Hills campaign
> Established a racial disdain that grew bigger:
> His lieutenants brought to Asia the stain that
> Called Philippine freedom fighters, *nigger*);

The Spanish American War: Annexation without Representation:
→ The Philippine-American War:
In the Philippine revolution to oust the Spanish,
Violent Americans came to banish revolutionary
Independence, and to rule a peaceful people
That had sought their sovereign own
Without any western terror sown, as the
    Balangiga Massacre is widely known,
Forty-eight Americans killed = 30,000 Filippino dead

Interlude: Armaments industries are digging new ground
    Promises of wealth in ways yet unfound!

World Wars:
a.k.a. The 20-year Armistice, cemented Mores
Where Might made Right, and sure before long the
Belligerent slogan: my country right or wrong!

    (Henry Ford's overseas peace commission
    Drew newspaper scorn and public derision,
    Instead of praise as peacemaking tools,
    They were ridiculed as a ship of fools);

The Korean War:
"Police Action" Arrogance soon met subsequent
Bay-of-Pigs "hit-the-beach" Romance upon which the
Official story is bent (visit any military museum);

The Vietnam War

Viet Cong vapors & Pentagon Papers all but ignored.
But at long last, Light leaked in and nationwide teach-ins
would underline the sacrifice of the Catonsville Nine;
more were willing to be gassed & arrested as passive
Resistance was continually tested. Finally, millions arose
to scream at Uncle Sam and ended the war in Vietnam!

> (Vets return to empower the schism, to
> Police the public they will serve
> Blue-blood masters' endemic racism:
> Divide and conquer will grade the curve);

Then there was peace, so to speak,
like grease applied upon a squeak.
Yet, active all the while,
American Arms Entrenched until Diabolical Deeds were
Recycled and Restored to await our next war, but
> for those unaware, do remember we have the
Rockets' Red Glare! And forget their flag,
Our Land Mines are still there for decade
Upon decade with data that floors,
> We are militarist whores!

People, we Must Arise and Make a Change, a
New national anthem we can arrange, for
Starters, a lifting tune with aimed content:
Singing the End of hegemony's evil intent!

    For many, our Collective Conscience Implores:
    End our role as militarist whores
    It behooves us one and all to
    Act to RESTORE the DIGNITY of the call:
        "LIBERTY and JUSTICE for ALL"
            viz.
    It's Time now America to Underscore

        WE HAVE HAD ENOUGH FOREVER WAR!

    OUT OF IRAQ! NO WAR W/ CHINA! WE MUST
REDUCE THE GLUTTONOUS MARTIAL BUDGET
      AND FOR THE GOOD OF ALL EMBRACE PEACE

Meanwhile, we face our deadliest foe
That All will Reap as All will Sow:

Climate Change:
American Military: how will you fight Climate Change?
Fire your missiles like killer bees to attack angry skies?
Launch ships and submarines against Uprising seas?
Specialists to attack ice? Siege permafrost at any cost?

In 2020, America had no $ to address climate change Facts. Since 2001, we'd spent **$14 Trillion** to go on the Attack in Wars in Afghanistan, Pakistan, and Iraq, and looking back, that's Billions of Tons of Greenhouse Military Gas passed by our *Guardians* as fossil fuels' global suicide-bomber acts!

The carbon footprint of our armed might
Is off the charts and out of sight:
The ozone layer is no barrier
Take for example, the aircraft carrier,

Each of these monsters of
Oil and Steel and Guns,
Cost a dozen billions for
100,000 tons!

Anchors aweigh with pomp unfurled
Feeds our insatiable Greed to
Export 'Liberty' around the World.

Add in those friggin' frigates at
One billion dollars each loading
Billion-dollar ballistic missiles
We use to teach 'Diplomacy.'

Also topping the billion-dollar ranks
Helicopters, trucks, jet fighters & tanks,
Submarines, cyberwar, and GPS satellites
All outbid the cost of, Pfffft, human rights!

We Need these weapons for the defense of
The teeming homeless sheltering in tents,
The needy, the hungry, the unemployed?
NO! To reimburse shareholder sangfroid!

While Joan & Jon Public
Spend the day shopping
    Celebrity news to
    Gossip of the times!
Frankly, they don't CARE
About their nation's past and
Present international crimes, they'd rather
Shop and surf the Net; there is so much more to Get!

Where was the nation's youth to protest our
Invented trespass when we invaded Iraq?
Their grandparents took to the streets
    Nationwide
With well-aimed anger & derision, yet 1991
    Saw but a few
Thousands in D.C. for one day, one place!

It was a Victory of
Complacency as marketed elision.
As long as *they* don't care and *few others* too,
Mobile Terror will go Anywhere, by air and
Through oceans and the Seven Seas or through
        ANY DOOR!
To feed the fire of creating enemies;
To perpetuate the fate our planet must either
Buffer or suffer from America the Great!

Gunited States
Part Two: Dream World Interlude

"Hope lies in dreams, in imagination, and in the courage of those who dare to make dreams into reality." —Jonas Salk

Can we turn defense contractors' output into ploughshares to

Help communities expand ideas of neighborhood?

    Not easily, but let us say YES! YES! YES!

Turn off the arms spigot! Let current deals circle drains,

What remains is Change, and in change some will

Lose jobs that others will gain, as in any rearrange:

Weaned from their habitual federal tit some corporations

Would fail is the long and the short of it, but we'd bail

Them out as we did the bank, the automaker or put them

On the dole while we alter America's role acre by acre

From international death exporter to global Peacemaker!

Bring back: The Works Progress Administration as a

Hybrid with the Civilian Conservation Corps & we will

Employ thousands of all ages for restoration that sews

Our crumbling country's urban texture, and Together

Working shoulder to shoulder, true Democracy grows

More than fifty-thousand bridges, water and sewer

Systems too are in dangerous states of disrepair, as

Well as railways, levees, public transit and schools

Because capitalism alone doesn't really care –

Note that old chestnut Tax Incentives too oft sold as

Ready fix whiz bang, they go like July 4th rockets!

Slogans fly, but the money heads to wealthy pockets

While the intended recipients reap but fool's gold.

The neo-liberal canard of government disinvestment

In public life is itself lard, as several generations have

Witnessed its halts and stumbles while all around,

Both above and underground, infrastructure crumbles.

Private business will never carry the weight of

Hundreds of thousands for betterment employed,

But with a new WPA a relatively inexpensive way

Will improve and upgrade lives and be by all enjoyed.

We have enough money – but it is in the wrong places,

But selling off or closing our foreign bases will reduce

Our carbon footprint, there's no better time than Now!

We the people will suffer to remove corporate rule from

Government: Throw off its traces and defang the ghoul!

When Americans Stand Together unsegregated and

Demand the Abrogation of Warfare Incorporated,

Then will gun gluttony wear a shameful face, a stated

About-face to a civilian army of Salvation determined to

Bind up and Salve this too-long wounded nation, but

Until such a time, our complacency will enable the

Agency of Forever War and extend the Endless

Domestic Shootings we ignore, while vigilantism

Parading as self-defense is used to settle scores!

Gunited States
Part Three: Gore in Our Lore

"The love interest in guns shows up in the American consciousness in the second half of the nineteenth century, product of the myth-making versions of what by the 1880s was no longer a lawless western frontier." —Lewis H. Lapham

Long before digital pixel guns
Toymakers thrived on marketing runs,
Kids had working triggers, rolls of caps,
Shootouts over stolen treasure maps

We played in fields, woods & city streets
Running, shooting & falling repeats,
Though in hindsight it appears appalling,
We were enacting our culture's calling,

When old enough for our first rifles
We wanted forty-fours, not trifles,
And looked askance at twenty-twos:
Inferior weaponry would lose,

German squirrels and Japanese frogs
Would prove no match in our backyard slogs,
We practiced popping bottles and cans, and
Improving the aim of our romance,

Crenelated castles, Dukes and Earls,
These were the days before we met girls,
Of the leaf fort, trench and sniper's nest
Our pre-testosterone lives attest,

But it wasn't all games, as we grew
TV programs regularly drew
Have Gun Will Travel, Combat, Gunsmoke:
Dramatic tale with an ethical yoke,

Back then, visuals weren't too graphic as
Vanilla pedestrian traffic:
Those shot fell down and lay quite still,
No special effects splatter and spill,

Some of us got on with life's main chore,
Coupling to raise a son or daughter, while
Others went off to spurious war and came
home petrified by senseless slaughter

Culture is a vulture, it is said,
It plays strange movies inside the head,
So that butchering children in school
Justifies flaunting gun freedom rule!

Given here is one example of gun
Lore in a media sample, looking
Ahead with backward roving eyes to
Our previous bloody centuries:

One image we randomly usurp is
The lionized lore of Wyatt Earp;
In building myth, he's a major girder,
That lawman got away with murder!

The bricks in the structure are made of
Hype, a grist of formulaic stereotype
And it's necessary to a degree
In crafting gunfighter pedigrees

An Eastern public keen to invest
Drove the sales of tales of the wild West,
Authors chose for their brag and bluster
Egotists like Earp and George Custer.

But amid the bluster one fact remains
Of an unarmed cowboy who was slain,
Due in part to his brother's morale
Shot in a lot leased by a corral,

Cinema treatment of the violent event
Ignores the trial Earp underwent,
He, his brothers, and one John Holiday
Charged with murder that October day.

The lion tarnished and in disgrace?
There were others that could take his place,
But truth lies fallow among the weeds:
It doesn't sell like fictional deeds;

Truth faces Myth on a dusty street,
One to vanquish, the other fleet;
Indoctrinated, we clearly see
The denouement choreography…

Two more killers with whom we're obsessed
Are Henry McCarty and mister J. James,
One from the heartland, one from the west,
Both of them ruined with deadly aims,

Both of them fought on the losing side,
Rebels: one with, one without a cause
And so established the killer bona fide,
Murdering people, defying laws:

To the pantheon elevated:
Earning our loftiest praise in lore:
Rise above those manipulated
And use a gun to settle the score:

To the pantheon elevated:
Celebrated in verse and in song,
Their deadly goals have escalated
Our WILLINGNESS to make right from wrong.

Dime novels were replaced as scripture by
The advent of the new motion picture,
Just as robbers, rustlers, and gunfighters
Got replaced by directors, screenwriters,

Gangster war, the new genre explored,
Internecine but leading toward
Acceptance of member-only deeds:
It's okay, then, to shoot up the streets?

As horse gave way to the motor car,
The silver screen featured mobster noir:
Dust bowl heroes the public abide,
Baby Face Nelson, Bonnie and Clyde,

Patterns emerged of stories retold,
The psychopath with a heart of gold,
A love affair with a lengthy run, the
Oath of silence, the machine gun,

We lapped it up and clamored for more,
More bullets than six guns boost the GORE,
We sat too rapt before the big screens
Gunners with choppers' drum magazines,

Stool pigeon, moll, and the verb, to finger,
Entered the lexicon and still linger
As grist for most gun-play romantics,
These images are driven by semantics:

Shotgun wedding and gunpowder teas,
Shooting the moon, shooting the breeze
Often conjures up friendly-fire ballistics
Amid volleys of rapid-fire linguistics!

Guns permeate a pop panegyric:
Nina Ross, Deuce Deuce, Fo' Fo, and Fo' Five,
Bust a cap, biscuit in hip-hop lyrics;
It's not only rhythm that keeps it alive:

We are a nation of blood-lust sheep
Whose abeyant conscience runs not deep
When kids are shot at school and at play
We bemoan, then turn one cheek away;

It's not so much that ethics is spurned
But that our love of gore's been Earned,
A badge worn on the metaphor sleeve:
Our core of blood and gore. Don't be naïve!

We're both promoters and purveyors
In pursuit of bottom dollar greed,
Con men, showboaters & surveyors;
Profit margins sanctify the deed;

Something must be done; we all proclaim,
While wringing our hands, assigning blame;
We agree only to disagree you see
On how we believe guns keep us free.

The Second Amendment out of context
Misconstrued with blatant derision; that
Purblind prevail to see what is next
With our limited human vision!

It's not too big a problem to solve,
But We Must Work Together if we
Expect to Move Forward and evolve;
Forever war is of similar issue and

> Wrapped around gun love like a braid,
> In our deep subcutaneous tissue: the
> Monster made must now be unmade:

The locus of wild West obsession
is bogus: Frontier wed Rampant Zeal,
Diverging from what was real. Their kids:
Pontificate, Exaggerate & Embellish
→forged myths that Today we relish;

We can undo the myth of the old West,
Unbuckling the gun belt's palimpsest:
Homesteaders struggling out on the plains,
Boredom and thirst on the wagon trains;

Violence random in occurrence
Not the fictive constant deference;
Focus on other depravity,
Ever before shown with brevity:

Gold rush frenzy and rowdy stampede,
Tin pan miner and the grubstake deed;
Theft of Indian Sacred Land as
Avarice of supply and demand.

Beware the revisionist rewrite,
Avoid typecast, cliché, reruns used
To demonize red, glorify white;
While we demythologize the gun.

That may stop when we no longer fill
Our ravenous appetite for waging war;
Our greatest goal must be to restore
Collective acts of moral good will!

Once divorced from the warrior romance.
Let us downsize armies, mothball some ships,
Perhaps then we will come out of our trance
And with surcease at last come to grips with

Shooting of children in their schools!
That should've been a wake-up call!
We have become a nation of Ghouls
Whose selective justice may ruin all!

~*~

The public police murder of George Floyd
    {and how many more before and since?}
Provoked millions who have howled & cried,
To Broadcast America's all but destroyed
E pluribus unum and how it is denied;

The murder of blacks by racist cops
Who've planted guns, then often lied,
Fraternities of public servant sops: the
Foremost faces of American Apartheid;

Socially constant since 1865,
Emancipation would never equate,
For each generation kept racism alive
Through systemic violence, covert hate.

~*~

Given the Enormity of our Duality:
    No Rational Argument:

Faces up to what our culture supports!
Excuses our hardwired terrorist role,
Pacifies lust for brutal cohorts, or
Brings to an End our grisly death toll,

It's a long road that we will Have to Go
To Redress the system, to Heed the Call,
To Abolish hatred & lynch Jim Crow,
    and gain Liberty & Justice for All;
As ONE we'll recast the American Dream,
Caring for an all-inclusive nation:
Sharing, bearing love, we will redeem our
Soul, and rejoice in righteous jubilation!

Afterword

Mythology gives us tools to help us understand the beliefs, stories, and traditions of cultures. Can the American mythos of the all-but-supernatural gunslinger and the soldier-sailor as savior help us come to grips with our devotion to firearms and the rationale of lethal force? Can it unpack our obsession with forever war? The poems in Gunited States respond with a resounding Yes!

As the title poem recommends, the monster we've made must now be unmade as we commit to better ourselves. In tracing our historic & symbolic narrative, these poems suggest how we can overcome our militaristic vigilante mindset, correct our moral failings, and extricate ourselves from the morass of mass murder.

Additional Reading

Lubet, Steven. *Murder in Tombstone: The Forgotten Trial of Wyatt Earp*. New Haven: Yale University Press, 2004

Ludwig, Jens. *Unforgiving Places: The Unexpected Origins of American Gun Violence*. University of Chicago Press, 2025.

McCoy, Alfred W. *Policing America's Empire: The United States, the Philippines, and the Rise of the Surveillance State*. University of Wisconsin Press, 2009.

Olsen, Steve. *False Gods: Why the Deification of Modern Conservatism Is Bad for America*. Lulu.com, 2011.

Silbey, David J. *A War of Frontier and Empire: The Philippine-American War, 1899-1902*. Hill and Wang, 2007.

Sjursen, Daniel A. *A True History of the United States: Indigenous Genocide, Radicalized Slavery, Hyper-Capitalism, Militarist Imperialism, and Other Overlooked Aspects of American Exceptionalism*. Steerforth Press, 2021.

Slotkin, Richard. *Gunfighter Nation: The Myth of the Frontier in Twentieth-Century America*. Norman: University of Oklahoma Press, 1998.

Smith, David Michael. *Endless Holocausts: Mass Death in the History of the United States Empire*. Monthly Review Press, 2023.

Wagner, Rachel. *Cowboy Apocalypse: Religion and the Myth of the Vigilante Messiah*. NYU Press, 2025

Steven Mooney's written work:

Poetry: *In Cellophane of Time, Poems 1973-1987*; *Harmony Rude*, 2025; *Mapping the Tongue*, 2026

Memoir, *Kottke Oeuvre Skookum, 6 & 12-string Ears, Vignettes, 1970-2019.*

Short Fiction, *Legend of Hyper Bole & other Stories.*

Miscellany, *A Brief History of Absolute Meat: Essays, Sketches, Stories*

Long Fiction: *Dalton Bourbonette*, a novel; and the comic-absurd novel trilogy, *Cutlass Wonders*; *The Ageless of Aquarius*; and *Chronicle of an English Morpheme Addict* with the overall title, *A Measure of Poe & Three Quarters*.

The series is available as a free download at Draft2Digital.com

www.ingramcontent.com/pod-product-compliance
Lightning Source LLC
Chambersburg PA
CBHW071012160426
43193CB00012B/2029